MARGARET SPOON

LIGHTER LIVING

The Essential Guide to Clutter-Free and Light Living , Learn Useful Ways on How to Declutter Your Life and Enjoy The Things That Really Matter To You

Descrierea CIP a Bibliotecii Naționale a României
MARGARET SPOON
   LIGHTER LIVING. The Essential Guide to Clutter-Free and Light Living , Learn Useful Ways on How to Declutter Your Life and Enjoy The Things That Really Matter To You / Margaret Spoon. – Bucharest: Editura My Ebook, 2020
   ISBN 978-606-983-590-6

MARGARET SPOON

LIGHTER LIVING

The Essential Guide to Clutter-Free and Light Living , Learn Useful Ways on How to Declutter Your Life and Enjoy The Things That Really Matter To You

My Ebook Publishing House
Bucharest, 2020

TABLE OF CONTENTS

Introduction 11

Chapter 1. **Begin with Acceptance** 15

Viewing Mistakes as Lessons 16

Don't Be Afraid to Admit Your Mistakes 17

Replacing Unhealthy Thoughts with Healthy Ones 18

Training Methods 19

Learning to Accept and Move On 20

Chapter 2. **Check Your Mindset** 22

Look Forward, Not Backwards 23

Give Yourself Credit 24

Goal-Oriented Mindset 25

Giving Yourself Time and Patience 27

When You Fail ……………………………….. 27

Lifelong Goals ……………………………… 28

Chapter 3. Unplug ……………………………….. 29

Unplug in the Morning …………………………. 31

Be the Boss of Your Weekend …………………... 33

Take Time Off – Completely …………………… 33

Go Off the Grid …………………………….. 33

Tech-Free Activities …………………………... 34

Live in the Moment ……………………………… 35

Chapter 4. How To Declutter Your Surroundings ….. 37

Set Time Aside ……………………………... 38

Where to Start ……………………………….. 38

Simplify Your Rooms …………………………… 39

Sorting Through ……………………………. 40

Make a Profit ……………………………... 41

Tackle the Closets 41

Your Work Area 42

Your Computer 43

Chapter 5. How To Put Daily Meditation Into Action 45

Meditation to Reduce Stress 46

Meditation for Better Energy 47

Meditation for Relaxation and Rejuvenation 47

Better Awareness and Focus 48

Better Patience 49

Oneness With the World 50

Meditation for Reduced Pain 51

Chapter 6. Practice Gratitude Daily 52

Develop Better Relationships 53

Improve Physical Health 53

Improve Mental Health 54

Increased Empathy and Sensitivity 54

Better Sleep 55

Improve Your Self Esteem 56

Increase Your Mental Strength 57

How to Practice Gratitude 58

Chapter 7. **Simplify Your Meal Plan** 59

Healthy Gut, Healthy Mind 60

Boost Your Brain Power 60

Happiness-Inducing Foods 61

Foods to Increase Serotonin 62

Eating More Vegetables 63

Active Cultures 64

Emotional Benefits of Eating Well 65

Chapter 8. **Organize Your Finances** 66

Decluttering Your Bank Account 67

Tackle Your Debt 68

Consolidating Your Debt 69

Save Money 70

Benefits of Organized Finances 71

Chapter 9. Remove Toxic People 72

Toxic People vs. Difficult People 73

Controlling 74

Disregard 74

Constant Taking 75

The Effects of Toxic People 75

Removing The Toxicity 76

Chapter 10. Creating a Personalized Plan
and Putting it Into Action 77

Conclusion & Recap 79

INTRODUCTION

What would you give to be happier? Do you have a lot of belongings, a large group of friends and a glowing career, but still don't seem to be able to find the inner peace and happiness that you long for?

All of us at some point have wished that we were happier. Whether we feel like our lives are running at far too fast a pace or stress is mounting up and becoming unbearable, there are many reasons for people to feel unhappy even in situations where it doesn't seem like they would have any reason to be.

In this book, you'll learn how to simplify your life to strip away the stress and as a result become happier and more fulfilled.

Do you want to learn how to accept your current situation and work with what you have to result in leading a happier life?

Do you want to learn how to live life happily without a constant need to be connected via electronic devices and understand how unplugging can actually help you to relax and de-stress?

Do you want to be able to unclutter your surroundings at home and work in a way that's so effective, it has a calming effect on your cluttered mind?

Is taking control of your diet and finances to become healthier and wealthier something that you'd love to do, but aren't quite sure how to muster up the motivation to get started?

Would getting rid of those toxic people in your life and all the drama which tends to unfold around them make you so much happier, but so far you haven't been able to get together the courage to cut them off?

In this book, you'll learn how to do all of this and more. Scaling back, simplifying your life, getting rid of the unnecessary and hanging on to the things that you're truly grateful for can help to lift your mood, eliminate stress and anxiety and make you feel much more motivated to be the best version of yourself and feel truly happy and content with what you have.

In this book, you'll learn how to:

- Accept and learn from your mistakes;

- Train your mind to replace negative thoughts with positive ones;

- Set and achieve your short and long term goals for happiness;

- Minimize stress;

- Create stronger relationships with family and friends by living in the moment;

- Take control of your own happiness;

- Reap the benefits of meditation;

- Be grateful more often;

- Choose foods that boost good mental health;

- Gain control of your finances, and

- Remove toxic people from your life.

Read on to discover how filling your life with extra stuff won't give you the inner peace that you crave – the answer is in simplicity.

CHAPTER 1

BEGIN WITH ACCEPTANCE

Before you can begin to transform your life into a simpler and happier journey, it's crucial that you learn to accept your current situation.

Acceptance doesn't mean that you'll need to learn to be completely happy with your lot – some situations you may never be able to feel completely satisfied with. Regrets are a natural

15

part of human life – after all, if you didn't make mistakes, you wouldn't be human, right?

Viewing Mistakes as Lessons

'Never a mistake, always a lesson learned' should be your life motto if you want to become skilled at accepting what you have. By viewing your mistakes as lessons learned, you'll experience less regret and guilt regarding the past and be able to better move on from your past experiences and practice full acceptance.

But with so many cultural assumptions about mistakes and failure, it can be difficult to see the mistakes which you've made in a positive light and use them to try and improve your future. Mainly, we are taught as people that mistakes are something to be ashamed of; schools, workplaces and even families encourage people to feel guilty about making mistakes and to do whatever they can in order to avoid them.

Combined with the inevitability of setbacks as a part of all aspects of life, this sense of shame provides an explanation for why many people, perhaps yourself included, give up on working to achieve their goals and suffer silent guilt and regret. What's missing in many people's beliefs is that setbacks and mistakes are actually a huge part of achieving any goal as they provide us with a learning experience and a basis of 'what not to do' for the future.

At the moment, your ultimate goal is to simplify your life and be happier. Before you can begin to achieve this goal successfully, it's vital that you change your opinion regarding setbacks and mistakes and cease viewing them as something which is shameful or bad. Instead, look on your mistakes and setbacks – both past and future – as not failures, but stepping stones to understanding yourself better and learning curves to get you on the right track to a happier and more fulfilled life.

Don't Be Afraid to Admit Your Mistakes

Admitting and accepting your mistakes is the first step towards viewing them in a new, positive manner. Dwelling on mistakes and looking at them in a negative way can create great feelings of guilt, regret and even shame which has a significant impact on your happiness and well-being.

Instead, it's important that you train yourself to accept your own inability to change the past. Letting go of your feelings regarding any mistakes you've made – whether you've gotten into debt, offended a close friend, messed up at work or made a bad decision in your life that's had a huge impact – is vital to moving forward and becoming a happier person.

Scaling back means simplifying your mind and removing those negative, toxic feelings regarding both past and future mistakes. Instead of thinking 'what if?' and dwelling on the 'could have, should have' part of a situation, channel your feelings into a more positive dimension.

Replacing Unhealthy Thoughts with Healthy Ones

Rather than thinking 'what would have happened if only I had done XX?', change your way of thinking when it comes to mistakes and past setbacks. Practice replacing your unhealthy thoughts with healthy ones until it becomes habit. For example:

Replace 'what if?', with 'what can I do now?' Replace 'if only…' with 'I accept the situation'.

Replace 'I shouldn't have done that' with 'I will learn from this to make sure I don't make the same decision again'.

Training your mind to accept your past mistakes and your current situation isn't something that happens overnight. If you are in a pattern of unhealthy thoughts of guilt and shame, it may take a lot of effort on your part to consciously make the decision to replace these thoughts with healthie ones. But, like any training, you will find that it gets easier as time goes on and you become used to being a more positive, happier person.

Training Methods

To help yourself effectively scale back the negative thoughts in your mind and replace them with positive ones, there are some methods of self-help and training which you may find useful. Many people find it extremely effective to get their thoughts out on paper. You could do this by writing down a list of the negative thoughts that you find yourself dwelling on regularly and writing positive 'replacement thoughts' alongside them. Keep the list in your wallet or purse or save it on your smartphone so that you can make a conscious effort to consult it when you start to experience negative thoughts that bring you down.

Wearing a snap band around the wrist is also an effective method which is endorsed by a number of psychologists and therapists. This method is quite simple; wear an elastic band around your wrist and gently snap it each time you feel yourself spiralling downwards into a negative mindset or feeling guilty and shameful regarding past mistakes which you can no longer control. The shock of the 'snap' sensation causes your mind to concentrate on something other than the feelings of negativity and can be the reminder you need to concentrate on a more positive view of the situation.

Learning to Accept and Move On

As you begin your journey of newfound positivity and acceptance, you will need to be prepared to meet setbacks. So far, your mind is caught in a cycle of negative, guilt and shame-inducing feelings and thoughts which are stealing from you the happiness which you want and deserve.

One of the worst mistakes that you can make is to believe that by learning to replace your negative thoughts with positive ones, you'll be immediately happy straight away. The road to happiness and contentment can be a long, winding one with many obstacles along the way – and often, the largest and most difficult of these obstacles exist in your own mind.

The truth is, acceptance and moving forward is never easy. You will be tempted every day to give some thought to your negative feelings and regrets. Instead of supressing these thoughts or feeling even more guilty about them, simply acknowledge them, and replace them. If you catch yourself wondering 'what if?' about a past decision, don't beat yourself up about it – after all, it's hard to crack a habit which you've been used to for so long.

Supressing negative feelings is unhealthy, which is why learning to acknowledge and accept these thoughts before making a conscious effort to replace them with healthier, positive and happier ones is vital to your own well-being and progress.

CHAPTER 2

CHECK YOUR MINDSET

Becoming a happier, more fulfilled and content person who exhibits positive energy and good vibes can only be achieved by one person: YOU.

Your mindset when you embark on the journey to scaling back and achieving a happier life is one of the most important factors which you need to take into serious consideration. Be honest with yourself – what is your mindset right now?

Do you feel positive and confident in yourself to make the changes that you need to in order to achieve your goals, or are you skeptical about the whole thing?

Do you rely on other people for your happiness and well-being, or can you accept that you as an individual are the only person responsible for this?

Entering into a plan for happiness with the wrong mindset is simply a recipe for disaster. Having the right mindset doesn't only include acceptance of mistakes as explained in the previous chapter, it also means that you'll need to transform your outlook on yourself and your own life and develop more confidence and security in your own ability to truly change your life for the better.

Look Forward, Not Backwards

Honestly, we don't care how many times you've screwed up before. You still have the rest of your life to make a difference and become a much happier person by scaling back and simplifying your life and your mind.

'Fall down seven times, stand up eight' – this should be your motto. Positive people don't give up on themselves, and they never view themselves as failures no matter how many setbacks they encounter on the journey to achieving their goals.

If you take the first step of this journey to happiness wholeheartedly believing that you're incapable and you'll never make it to the finish line, you're already setting yourself up for failure. Instead, start learning to believe in yourself. Change your mindset to start with a 'can-do' attitude. Give yourself the benefit of the doubt – after all, if you weren't serious about becoming a happier person, you wouldn't be reading this book!

Give Yourself Credit

Many unfulfilled, unhappy people are that way due to the fact that they never give themselves enough credit where credit is due.

There's nothing wrong with always wanting to push yourself further, and self-criticism can be absolutely healthy and even motivating – but if you have gotten to the point where your self-criticizing thoughts and beliefs are taking over and you never allow yourself believe that you've actually done anything right, it's time to take a step back and re-evaluate your self-treatment.

Allowing yourself some praise and recognition for achievements which you are proud of is essential when you're on the path to scaling back and becoming happier. Not only should you be scaling back the things in your life that take your happiness and inner peace away, it's also crucial that you cut down on the amount of self-criticizing thoughts which you have and allow yourself to replace them with self-motivating and self-appraising thoughts. There's absolutely nothing wrong with being proud of yourself, whether it be for getting through a day without feeling regret regarding the past or successfully completing a six-month healthy living plan.

Goal-Oriented Mindset

The aim of the game is to simplify and scale back in order to become more content, happier and find your inner peace with yourself, your life and the world. Think about that for a second – it's a huge goal! Many people spend all of their lives searching for the happiness which you're trying to achieve, and a lot of people never find it because they have the wrong mindset.

Having a goal-oriented mindset is absolutely essential when you begin this interesting and emotional journey.

Setting your sights on the one, huge end-goal is likely to be very overwhelming. If you're currently living an unhappy life with negative thoughts and feelings, regret, guilt, shame, stress and worry, setting one massive goal of 'achieving happiness' is going to seem a hundred million miles away.

The key to obtaining your goal is to do so by creating a set of mini-goals which you should view as stepping stones to your ultimate goal of a happier life. As you read on, you'll discover more about the types of goals which you could set in order to make the journey easier on yourself.

Once you've set your goals – either by using this book as a guide, creating personal goals tailored to yourself or a mixture of the two – you should check your mindset as you go through them. Do you believe in yourself and the fact that you can achieve these goals? How are you approaching these goals? If you approach them with a negative mindset and no self-confidence, you will be disappointed with the results.

Giving Yourself Time and Patience

Achieving goals in your personal life which pertain to your own happiness should be something that is done at your own pace. Never let anybody else tell you how long you should be spending on each goal – it isn't their place to say, and only you know how much time you need to change a part of your life or your mindset.

Don't approach your goals with strict deadlines, as this will only encourage negative feelings and guilty emotions if you don't achieve the goal within the time-frame that you have set for yourself. Instead, be patient with yourself and recognize the fact that you may need time to transform your mindset and emotions in order to effectively make the changes needed in your life to fully achieve a goal. Slow and steady wins the race – ultimately, your mindset should always be about making effective changes in your life rather than quick ones.

When You Fail

If you don't achieve a goal or find yourself slipping backwards, don't panic. Perhaps you've come close to achieving your goal of changing your eating plan and exercising daily, for example, only to find yourself slipping back into your old habits of sitting in front of the television with a pizza and fries. This is perfectly OK, and normal! Never beat yourself up for setbacks – they are an important part of achieving your goals. Instead, think about how your period of relapse made you feel – did you feel happier, or could you feel the old, negative thoughts and unhappiness creeping back? Allow this to be what motivates you and spurs you on to achieve the goal you have set for yourself.

Lifelong Goals

If you have the mindset that the goals you're setting for yourself when it comes to scaling back have a time-frame or deadline attached to them, you'll be disappointed.

Unfortunately, there'll be no 'magic day' where you'll suddenly fully achieve a goal and never look back again. Set-backs and relapses are bound to happen, and there will be days where you can't help but feel unhappy and negative about things. It's all part of human life – nobody can be completely happy all of the time! However, setting life-long goals to use as a guide can help you to take control of your negativity and unhappiness rather than allowing these feelings and emotions to have control over you.

CHAPTER 3

UNPLUG

Are you glued to your electronic devices? Do you find yourself spending more time communicating with friends and family over instant messaging or text message rather than meeting up and spending quality time in person?

There's no denying that technology is changing the way that we live. Currently, we're living in the digital revolution where smart technology is playing a huge part in the way we communicate, shop, and complete tasks amongst many things.

By advising that you 'unplug', we're not suggesting that technology isn't beneficial. In fact, quite the opposite – technology can help to lift your mood by putting you in touch with old friends and family, providing lines of communication to important people who enrich and fulfil your life, and giving you the opportunity to learn new things.

However, the downside to technology is that it can often create a disconnect from the real world. Studies show that the average smartphone user checks their device six times an hour – and if you're checking for just five minutes at a time, that's a full half of your twelve-hour day spent on your smartphone.

With that in mind, it's little wonder that many people today are feeling stressed out and overwhelmed. Six hours per day is a long time to spend checking your smartphone – and that's without added gadgets and devices such as tablets, laptops, and televisions!

What makes matters worse is that we're the ones who are constantly interrupting ourselves, constantly feeling the urge to check our smartphones and other devices when they buzz or even when they don't. What is this constant influx of information doing to us as people? It's creating a world where people are stressed out, running out of time to get things done, exhausted and perpetually on the brink of catching a cold or even worse due to their fried, tired-out immune systems. This isn't a healthy recipe for happiness.

Unplug in the Morning

If your morning routine involves checking your smartphone for half an hour, logging straight onto your email or switching the television on, stop. Scaling back to make your morning routine simple, refreshing and relaxing is key to getting a great start to the day and will set you up for a happy, relaxed and positive state of mind all day long.

In the morning, try to avoid technology and gadgets as much as possible. Instead, go about your morning routine and enjoy the calm and quiet which comes with no television blaring or smartphone buzzing with notifications every few minutes. Rather than spending thirty minutes checking your smartphone when you awaken, use the time to do something which will contribute to a calmer state of mind such as meditation, enjoying a longer shower or eating a healthy, nutritious breakfast.

Sure, switching off all gadgets and devices in the morning might not help you earn brownie points from your kids if you're a parent, and at the beginning you might even hate it too. But, by lowering the level of distraction in the morning as well as keeping the noise down, you'll soon begin to appreciate the calming of early morning chaos and being able to begin your days without being stressed out before your feet even hit your bedroom rug.

Be the Boss of Your Weekend

Does your boss enjoy spending his entire Sunday morning firing off work- related emails? Sure, if he wants to fill his weekend with work then that's his choice, but it doesn't mean that you're obliged to answer. Unless you work in national security or have lives depending on you there's no reason why you should need to reply or even check work-related emails until business hours resume as normal. With the digital revolution making it easier than ever for everyone to stay connected all the time, setting boundaries has never been more important. Responding to weekend emails that you're not being paid to read will give your boss the impression that you're on call – definitely something you don't need!

Take Time Off – Completely

It's important to make weekends and vacation days a time for true relaxation and disconnect from work rather than just being diluted-down versions of your regular workday. Schedule your out-of-office emails for when you're not working, and resist the urge to check your email account and respond to any emails until just a few hours before you're set to return. If you can't avoid checking emails, inform your colleagues that you'll only be checking email at certain times during your vacation days and will only reply to urgent ones if absolutely necessary.

Leaving work at the office and switching off your business phone and laptop when you get home can help your mind to refresh and relax.

Although at times being connected to your job from home may be unavoidable, it's important to value your off-time as working too much can leave you feeling stressed and burned out.

Go Off the Grid

Going off the grid might not be a feasible option for some people, but if you can afford to take some time away from the hustle and bustle of daily life for a couple of days technology-free, you should definitely go for it.

Use your tech-free time to do something which will enrich your body and soul and help to restore your happiness and inner peace, leaving you feeling rejuvenated and revitalized. For example, you might consider taking a relaxing spa weekend alone and leaving your smartphone behind, or even spending a couple of days exploring nature through walks or sunbathing on the beach. The peace and tranquillity you'll get from being alone and not having the pressure of your smartphone there at all times will help you to clear your mind.

Of course if you're planning to go off the grid it's important to let somebody know where you'll be and when to expect you back. Although leaving your smartphone behind is ideal, if you won't have any other way of contacting family or friends in an emergency, you may need to take it along – just leave it switched off as long as you can!

Tech-Free Activities

One of the simplest and easiest ways to start scaling back your technology use on your pathway to becoming a happier person is to take up activities which you can't use your smartphone or another device when you're participating. Activities such as hiking, swimming, yoga and meditation are all utterly incompatible with electronic devices, and they can also help towards making you feel better about yourself and happier on their own.

Live in the Moment

Many pictures, memes and videos on the topic of smartphones stopping us from living in the moment have gone viral online – ironically from the amount of people viewing them on their smartphones.

But, it's definitely true – people these days tend to do everything from behind the screen of a smartphone whether it be communication or even viewing events that are unfolding right in front of them. Think about it – if you were to see something completely amazing right in front of you, what would be the first thing that you'd do? If you're like most people on the planet today, it's be to reach for your smartphone to take a photo or video and upload it to social media.

The truth is that whilst being able to create awesome memories and keep them permanently is a wonderful thing, there needs to be a balance somewhere between capturing the moment and living in it. Limit your 'capturing the moment' scenarios to things that really deserve to be captured, and start living in the moment more often – for example by putting your smartphone away and leaving it there when you're out for dinner with friends.

If your family and close friends seem to be a little distant with you recently or annoyed with your lack of attention, it could be the screen that's coming between you that's hugely contributing to the problem. Learning to put your smartphone down and give people your full attention can significantly impact your happiness and well-being.

HOW TO DECLUTTER YOUR SURROUNDINGS

Excessive clutter is often a main symptom of stress and can even cause stress. An excessively cluttered environment can affect every aspect of your life from the time it takes you to complete tasks to the state of your finances and your general well-being and overall enjoyment and quality of life.

Clutter can distract you and weigh you down both mentally and physically. In general, clutter does nothing but simply invites chaos into your life and the environment where you live it. But, tackling the clutter can seem like a task which is completely insurmountable if you're not sure where or how you should start.

Set Time Aside

The best way to approach the de-cluttering of your home is to look at it as a series of small tasks rather than one massive one. Setting aside a huge chunk of time to be dedicated simply to the purpose of decluttering could leave you exhausted and perhaps even feeling stressed, which is why it's a far better option to take small steps. Set aside an hour or two each day at a time where you are feeling the most motivated and energized in order to tackle the clutter and free up space in your home and work environment.

Where to Start

If you have a lot of clutter, knowing where to start could be a difficult decision. In general, it's best to start in those places where you spend the most time, such as the bedroom, living room or your work space. Make a list in order of spaces where you spend the most time and would benefit the most from the area being de-cluttered.

Simplify Your Rooms

Once you have decided where you are going to start the task of decluttering, simplifying your rooms is the first thing that you'll need to concentrate on. No matter which room you begin with, freeing up space and turning it into a clear, tidy haven which won't add stress and anxiety to your mind and mood is the main goal.

Begin by clearing anything which is on the floors of the room – you'll immediately begin to see a difference, especially if there are lots of items laying around on the floor. If storage is an issue, it might be a good idea to look for smart storage solutions such as under-bed storage where you can safely keep any items that you can't throw away out of sight.

Once you've cleared the floor, move on to flat surfaces such as counter tops, tops of dressers, shelves etc. You should clear them of clutter as much as possible – in general, these are the areas in a living space which are susceptible to the most clutter, as many people mindlessly just put items on top of them meaning that they can soon get full up of items that in most cases, you might not really need. Go over all your flat surfaces with a fine tooth comb and be ruthless – if it's something that you barely ever use, throw it away! After you've tackled the flat surfaces, the next step is to clear clutter from any furniture, cabinets and cupboards.

Sorting Through

Sorting through items to determine what needs to be kept and what you can get rid of can be a bit of a mammoth task. This can be even worse if you've accumulated a lot of things over the years, so having a system in place to help to make the decision to keep or not is important.

When you're sorting through your things, the best way to tackle it is to have three different piles. Firstly, you'll have the 'keep' pile, where you'll put everything that you need and aren't able to throw or give away. Secondly, have a 'donate' pile, where you can put those items that you can give to others such as friends and family, thrift stores or even give to charity.

Lastly, have a 'throw away' pile for items that you can't keep or give away – these can simply go in the trash. Make sure to keep the piles of items neatly organized and uncluttered –

using storage boxes or refuse sacks to keep your different piles of items separate is a great plan.

Make a Profit

If you want to make some money from your decluttering project, add a fourth pile to your sorting system. This is the 'sell' pile, where you can put anything that you don't need any more but might be able to sell on to make some money. Clothing which is in good condition, old gadgets that still work, children's toys and even miscellaneous items such as DVDs can all make for great garage sales or you could even list them on sites such as eBay. Making money from your unwanted items and clutter can be a great idea – just make sure that you don't end up spending your profits on more! Instead, use the money for something that you can use to improve your happiness such as a quiet weekend break, yoga lessons, or put it into your savings account.

Tackle the Closets

When you're clearing through your home, don't forget to tackle all your closets. Because closets are some of the best places to store things out of view, they can easily become cluttered up as you shove items in them to free up space in the bedroom. Clothes that you don't wear any longer can also have your closets packed full – making it more difficult to find the items that you do want to wear.

This can lead to stress in the morning when you can't find the outfit that you need whilst you're getting ready for work! Set aside time to go through your closets and take out any items which don't really belong there. Then go through your clothes – be ruthless, keeping only the garments which you wear often and like. If you haven't worn something for months – with the exception of special occasion wear – it's likely that you won't wear it again, or miss it when it's gone.

Your Work Area

Whether your work area is at home, at an office outside of the home or you have a work area for both, keeping it free of clutter is essential. Your work area is where you spend a large portion of your day, and an untidy, cluttered desk can cause chaos and add to your stress levels and anxiety at work.

To get started with your work area, begin with the desk surface. Desks can get dusty and dirty quickly, so before you begin to sort through the items stored in and on your desk, the best thing to do is clear everything off it and wipe it down so that you've got a nice, clean area to work with.

Assemble all of the items found on and in your desk on the floor, and sort them into piles to determine what you need and what you can throw out. If you have a lot of papers on your desk, shred anything that you don't need any longer – you'd be surprised at how much space paper can take up! Aim to go paperless as much as possible by storing electronic versions of files instead.

Labelling things on your desk can make it much easier to navigate and keep on top of. Designate drawers for different items or projects, and set up a basic alphabetic filing system. Try to keep flat surfaces as clear as possible and have an inbox system for all incoming papers so that they don't get tossed on your desk.

Your Computer

Lastly, take a look at your computer and see if that needs to be decluttered as well. Get rid of any files and programs which you no longer need or use, and set up an easy-to-use filing system on your computer so that you can access files which you need quickly.

You'll also be surprised at how much faster your computer will run once you've deleted any unnecessary files and programs – slow running computers tend to add to a lot of stress at work, so keeping it clear of clutter can help your work day run more smoothly.

HOW TO PUT DAILY MEDITATION INTO ACTION

Now you have decluttered your physical surroundings, it's time to begin to begin the process of decluttering your mind. Although a tidy, clean home and work space which is free from clutter can immediately help to reduce stress and make you feel happier, it's the clutter in your mind which can cause you to fall short of reaching your goal of being a happier person.

Daily meditation is essential if you're committed to decluttering your thoughts, learning to handle your emotions more effectively and being more in touch with your inner self.

Meditation to Reduce Stress

One of the main benefits of practicing regular mindfulness meditation is that it can have a significant impact on your stress levels. People who meditate daily find that over time, their levels of stress and feelings of anxiety begin to noticeably drop, leading them to a calmer, more peaceful and controlled mindset. Meditating every day helps you begin to see things differently, and by doing it each day consistently for a couple of months or even just a few weeks, you'll soon find that you are feeling less stressed and worried and are able to handle situations a lot better.

Regular meditation causes things which may have seemed very important before to not be so, and what you may have considered stressful in the past will no longer be as you'll be in better control of your own mind and able to handle anything that life throws at you. This is because when you meditate, you begin to understand that your own well-being is much more important than events or material things, causing you to put less emphasis on them and more emphasis on looking after yourself and your own happiness.

Meditation for Better Energy

If you are feeling tired and run down, meditation can be the perfect cure. When you make daily meditation a regular habit, you will have access to an abundant source of energy as you learn techniques such as opening your crown chakra to allow the source of energy to flood your whole body. The energy which you gain from meditation gives you more power, control, and cleanses your nerves, allowing you to no longer suffer from feeling drained in the middle of the day or feeling tired after just a small amount of work.

Meditation for Relaxation and Rejuvenation

Daily meditation is an excellent habit if you are currently unable to sleep well. Stress and anxiety can cause even the most tired of minds to work overtime, and if you're unhappy, you're not likely to be getting a deep and fulfilling sleep each night. If you are waking up feeling unrefreshed each morning and the stress of your life is causing you to toss and turn each night, the habit of daily meditation has the answers that you need.

When you practice regular meditation, your body learns to be able to completely relax, and you will have better control over your thoughts meaning that you will no longer suffer from such a great amount of thoughts in your head. Due to this increased relaxation and better mind control, you will be able to fall asleep much easier at night as well as have a deeper and more refreshing sleep.

Not only that, but the better sleep which you will be experiencing as a result of meditation along with the energy that you receive from your habit will rejuvenate your body as well as your mind. Your mood will also be raised, in turn making your body look younger – when you meditate daily, it's not uncommon to hear compliments from others about how much healthier and happier you look.

Better Awareness and Focus

Daily meditation raises you to a higher level of awareness. This is one of the main benefits of meditation for people who are very unhappy or even suffering from depression, and those with low levels of awareness often find it difficult to easily control their emotions and can be easily influenced by the emotions of other people.

Achieving a higher level of awareness means that you will feel more centred, happy and peaceful. In general, higher awareness will help to improve your life in a number of different ways, and you'll find that situations and things which once scared or worried you will no longer have such a significant impact on your well-being.

Daily meditation can also help you if you have a short attention span and find it difficult to stay focused and concentrated on one thing for an extended period of time. Meditation in itself requires you to stay in the same position for fifteen minutes or more, clear your head from thoughts and remain focused on the act of meditation itself.

When you get used to doing this, you'll find that your focus will also improve when it comes to the other areas of your life.

Better Patience

Since meditation requires you to remain quiet and in the same position for around fifteen minutes at a time, it won't only improve your focus and awareness, it'll also have an impact on your patience levels. Having the patience to deal with stressful situations is important when you want to achieve your goal of being happier.

After a couple of weeks of practicing daily meditation, you will notice that your patience is increasing. You will no longer feel frustrated during situations such as when driving in heavy traffic or when you are in a long queue at the store.

Oneness With the World

Everyday meditation will enable you to feel a better sense of oneness with everything in the world. A large portion of the misery and upset in society is caused as a result of people not feeling at one with others and their surroundings. However, meditation will help you to understand how everything in the world is connected. Everything and everybody is simply energy at different densities, and practicing meditation will help you to better feel the connection that you have with the world and everything in it.

Once you reach this understanding of oneness, you will feel much happier, relaxed, and be able to judge others less and form better and more meaningful relationships. This feeling of oneness can also help you to feel much closer to nature, something which can make you feel happier in and of itself.

Meditation for Reduced Pain

Suffering from aches and pains can greatly decrease from the happiness and fulfilment that you feel. Nobody likes to go about their everyday life whilst suffering from joint and muscle pain or headaches, for example, and in many cases, daily meditation can be a more effective cure than taking painkiller medications.

Headaches are often caused by stress, and with stress being a result of having too many thoughts in your head at once, meditation helps as it causes you to put unnecessary thoughts out of your mind and get rid of the mental clutter. When practicing meditation daily, you will no longer be thinking as many thoughts at once and therefore any headaches caused by stress and anxiety will disappear. Since meditation helps your muscles to relax, it can help reduce or completely eliminate muscle pain.

CHAPTER 6

PRACTICE GRATITUDE DAILY

Saying 'thank you' is something that we tend to do automatically – when somebody holds a door open, or if somebody lets us pass on the sidewalk for example. But, there's a difference between just uttering the words 'thank you' and actually practicing a grateful attitude. Instead of saving being thankful for simply those times of year where it's popular such as

Thanksgiving or the Christmas season, practicing an attitude of gratitude every day of your life can open up a number of benefits to you and your happiness.

Develop Better Relationships

Not only does practicing gratitude and saying thank you constitute good manners, studies show that displaying appreciation can actually be a great way to make and retain new friends. Thanking a new acquaintance increases the likelihood of them wanting to pursue an ongoing relationship. So, whether you thank a work colleague for holding a door open for you or write a quick note expressing gratitude to somebody who helped you on a project, acknowledging other people's contributions towards your life and happiness can lead to new opportunities.

Improve Physical Health

Expressing gratitude can have a significant effect on your physical health. Reports show that grateful people tend to experience less aches and pains and feel healthier than people who don't practice gratitude regularly.

Perhaps unsurprisingly, practicing regular gratitude will also encourage you to take better care of your own health for example by exercising regularly and visiting the doctor for frequent health check-ups. Being grateful for what you have regarding your health can be a great motivator when it comes to paying more attention to looking after yourself.

Improve Mental Health

Practicing gratitude can seriously help to improve your mental and emotional health. Being truly thankful can decrease a significant number of unhealthy and negative emotions which you may feel, for example anger, resentment, regret envy or frustration.

Leading researchers in the study of gratitude have proven with a number of different case studies that making a conscious effort to practice gratitude daily can have a huge positive impact on your well-being, helping to improve happiness and minimizes feelings of anxiety, depression and dissatisfaction.

Increased Empathy and Sensitivity

People who practice gratitude daily and truly learn to be thankful for what they have also experience an increased ability to be sensitive to others and empathize with them. When you are not in the habit of practicing gratitude, it can be easy to behave in a revengeful manner and hold grudges – all of which can strip away from your overall happiness and well-being.

Being grateful will help you to behave in more of a prosocial manner, even when others behave less kindly to you. Having the ability to empathize with others will put you in a position where you are less likely to retaliate against others and be able to see the positive side of situations more often.

Practicing gratitude can significantly decrease your desire to seek revenge even when others wrong you, which in turn helps you to let go of negative and stressful thoughts which can interfere with your happiness.

Better Sleep

It is no secret that not sleeping well can have a huge impact on how happy you feel in your daily life. Sleep is vital to our mental energy and getting a good night's rest enables you to start each day feeling refreshed, rejuvenated and ready to take on any stress and complications which may get in your way.

Practicing gratitude reduces negative thoughts of stress, worry, envy, anxiety and even revenge – all of the things which can keep you up at night. Studies show that grateful people tend to get a much better sleep each night as they don't have as many negative thoughts and feelings in their mind preventing them from relaxing and falling into a deep and refreshing sleep. Spending just ten to fifteen minutes jotting down a few things which you are grateful for before bed can help to increase your happiness and allow you to sleep feeling significantly more positive and relaxed.

Improve Your Self Esteem

When you practice gratitude on a daily basis, you will automatically become a nicer and more positive person – something which can significantly improve your self-esteem. If up until now your life has been cluttered with stress, dissatisfaction and unhappiness, it's highly likely that your self-esteem will also be suffering as a result.

When you practice gratitude, you will be a lot less likely to experience feelings of resentment towards people in better careers, for example. This will in turn encourage you to feel content with your own life and the things which you have – something which is crucial for good self-esteem.

Comparing yourself to others can cause you to foster resentful and negative feelings towards yourself. However, daily gratitude can help these feelings to disappear and instead, you will begin to foster feelings of thankfulness for what you have and a pride in yourself for everything which you have achieved.

Increase Your Mental Strength

Being stronger mentally is yet another of the benefits which you will experience when you begin to practice the habit of daily gratitude. Over the years, extensive research of people who engage in daily gratitude has not only shown that the habit is able to reduce stress and increase happiness, it can also play a major part in helping individuals to overcome trauma.

Experiencing a traumatic event whether it be in childhood or adult life is a huge contributor to feeling unhappy in your daily life. Recovering from trauma can take years, and in many cases it is a person's mindset which decides how quickly and how well they discover, regardless of any help or treatment which they are receiving in order to assist in their recovery.

If you have been through trauma in your life, practicing daily gratitude can help you to quicken your recovery and gain better control over your life and emotions. Recognizing all of the things which you have to be grateful for even during the worst times of your life leads to a greater ability to foster resilience and strengthen your mind, putting you in a better position to cope with trauma.

How to Practice Gratitude

We all have the ability to cultivate and practice gratitude. However, if you currently feel that you have nothing to be thankful for and have hit rock bottom, it can be extremely difficult to begin changing your habits to practice gratitude daily and be thankful for everything which you have.

But, it's important that you don't give up. Ensure that you use the positive mindset and strategies for practicing acceptance that were mentioned in the first two chapters when you are working to increase your ability to practice gratitude each day. You could begin by simply taking a few minutes each day in which you will make the effort to list some things which you are grateful for.

This doesn't have to be huge things – the small things can often mean the most, so if you're grateful that it didn't rain today, you're practicing gratitude. As you get used to finding things to be thankful for rather than finding things to resent, you will become more used to the habit and eventually, practicing gratitude will become second nature.

CHAPTER 7

SIMPLIFY YOUR MEAL PLAN

Have you ever heard the saying 'you are what you eat'? The foods and drinks which you put into your body can have a huge effect on your happiness and mental well-being.

It isn't just your physical health which can be improved by simplifying and improving your meal plan – by doing so, you'll also be able to choose foods that can actively heighten your positive mental state and improve your outlook on life.

Healthy Gut, Healthy Mind

You've probably heard about eating well to improve your physical health and reduce the risk of heart attack, diabetes, stroke and other conditions – but did you know that eating well can also reduce your risk of mental health conditions such as depression and anxiety?

Simplifying your meal plan and making smart changes to the foods which you eat can help to boost cognitive function and reduce symptoms of depression, causing your mood to be lifted and increase your feelings of happiness and contentment.

Boost Your Brain Power

When most of us think about boosting our brain power, diet is probably the last thing to come to mind. For most of us, the idea of boosting brain power and increasing cognitive function is something which we might do by participating in a thought-provoking debate or perhaps even playing 'brain-training' games. However, it turns out that one of the best ways to improve your mental health is through your diet. Just like the brain, your gut has its own nervous system which sends information to your brain via the vagus nerve. This explains why it's common to feel queasy or nauseous when you're stressed or worried. Just as the brain can impact the gut, your gut can also influence your brain.

Happiness-Inducing Foods

You might think that comfort foods such as cake are the best to opt for if you want to feel happier, but the truth is that whilst eating these kinds of foods might help you to feel more satisfied for a short period of time, they do little to improve your permanent mental well-being over time.

When you're choosing foods to include in your diet, some are much better than others when it comes to having an effect on your happiness, well- being and mental health. Fatty fish which are high in Omega-3, for example, are essential to proper and healthy functioning of the brain. If like most Americans your diet is deficient in omega-3 fatty acids and high in trans and saturated fats, this could be a huge reason for stress and even feelings of depression. Our brains are made up largely of fat and our bodies cannot manufacture essential fatty acids on their own, meaning that we rely heavily on it in our diets.

Studies show that foods which are high in these fatty acids such as cold water fish have been shown to decrease symptoms of a number of mental health disorders such as major depressive disorder, attention deficit hypersensitivity disorder and even schizophrenia.

Foods to Increase Serotonin

Often referred to as 'Nature's Prozac', the neurotransmitter known as serotonin has a direct effect on mental health. The foods which we include in our diets are broken down into substances which make neurotransmitters and other chemicals that allow different parts of the human nervous system to communicate effectively not only with just each other, but also with the rest of the body. The proper production of these chemicals and substances is vital to good mental health and subsequently, your happiness.

Next to carbohydrates, protein is one of the most important and abundant substance in your body. The amino acid tryptophan is a building block of protein that plays a vital part in influencing mood by producing the serotonin neurotransmitter. Serotonin is commonly associated with depression, and it's a medical fact that imbalances of serotonin levels in the brain can significantly contribute to feelings of depression, anxiety and general unhappiness.

Lean protein sources, such as chicken, fish, turkey, beans and eggs are all fantastic foods to include in your diet if you want to eat in such a way that the serotonin in your brain is balanced. Even more important are complex carbohydrates – food such as rice or brown pasta – which actually facilitate the entry of tryptophan into the brain. Eating more of these foods can relieve the symptoms of depression and anxiety as well as improve your overall cognitive function.

Eating More Vegetables

When your parents told you to eat your greens as a child, they certainly had good reason. Leafy green vegetables such as broccoli, spinach, romaine lettuce, mustard greens, beet and lentils are all high in folic acid, a substance which is linked directly to conditions such as depression, insomnia and fatigue.

If your diet is deficient in folic acid, you're more likely to feel depressed, have less energy or struggle to sleep at night. When you are putting together your simplified diet plan, it's vital to include lots of leafy greens which are high in folic acid into your meals in order to engineer a plan that significantly contributes to your happiness and well-being.

Broccoli is a food which contains selenium, a trace mineral which plays a highly important function when it comes to our immune systems, metabolism of the thyroid hormones and even reproduction. Some studies have suggested that low levels of this mineral in the body can contribute to feelings of depression and anxiety as well as a lack of energy and fatigue. Other food sources of selenium include onions, chicken, seafood, whole-grain food and some nuts such as brazil nuts and walnuts – all of which can be easily incorporated into a new, healthier diet.

Active Cultures

Yogurt doesn't only make a healthy snacking option. Yogurts which are high in active cultures contain probiotics, healthy bacteria which studies have shown to have a direct correlation with the reduction of stress and anxiety by affecting the neurotransmitter GABA.

In contrast to this, eating too much processed food which don't include these probiotics can significantly affect the delicate balance of healthy and unhealthy bacteria in the gut, something which can actually cause you to feel more stressed and anxious. Making healthy choices and removing the clutter of processed and unhealthy foods from your diet doesn't only aid your physical health, it also provides your body with the nutrients it needs to improve your mental health, happiness and well-being.

Emotional Benefits of Eating Well

The physical benefits of simplifying and improving your diet have a direct correlation to your emotions. When you eat healthily and take care of your diet, your physical health will improve and you will feel a lot more energetic. The extra motivation and energy which you will gain from eating well can help to reduce symptoms of stress and encourage you to feel less run- down, tired and fatigued during the day. Choosing healthier options can also aid you with weight loss, and losing weight brings along with it a range of further benefits such as increased confidence in yourself and a better self-esteem.

CHAPTER 8

ORGANIZE YOUR FINANCES

Your financial situation can have a direct effect on your happiness. Stressing about money is one of the main things which decreases calm, induces anxiety and depression and keeps people up at night.

Getting your finances in order and decluttering your bank account is a move which will play a major factor in achieving your goal of scaling back and becoming a happier person. Everybody's financial situation is different, but for the most part, many people spend a lot of time worrying about how much money they have and other financial problems such as repaying debts.

Finances may not be a major problem in the life of some individuals, and in some cases, your money may not be a factor which is contributing to any of your stress or unhappiness. But, if you find that worrying about money is taking up a large chunk of your time, it's vital that you get control.

Decluttering Your Bank Account

When was the last time that you went through all of the payments which are scheduled to go out of your bank account each month? A large number of people make unnecessary payments each month – these could be old insurance payments that you don't need any longer, or even payments to a gym or fitness club which you no longer attend. Making these payments is literally equivalent to throwing money down the drain and puts you out of pocket, contributing to your stress regarding your finances.

Go through your bank account with a fine tooth comb, and cancel any payments which you no longer need to make. You may be surprised at the amount that you're actually paying out when it all adds up and depending on the number of payments that you cancel, you could save yourself a significant amount of money which can then be put towards savings or other expenditures.

Tackle Your Debt

Debt is a major cause of worry and stress for many individuals. Paying off debts can be stressful, and the anxiety can become even more severe if you miss or struggle to keep up with repayments and begin to get calls and letters from your creditors reminding you that you need to pay the money back – often with a late repayment charge added on the top.

If debts are currently stealing away your happiness and calm, the best thing to do is tackle them head on and take control. Rather than try to ignore your debts and push them to the back of your mind, facing the debt and doing what you can to gain control back over your finances is more effective when it comes to improving your happiness.

Ignoring your debts may help you to feel less stressed for a short time, but these feelings of stress and anxiety will soon return at an even higher level when your creditors begin to chase the money that you owe them. Rather than put your debt worries to the back of your mind, be proactive and call your creditors to alert them to your situation and come to an agreement which works well for both parties and doesn't contribute to your stress.

Consolidating Your Debt

If debt worries are getting you down, you should explore the range of different options available to you that allow you to consolidate or even reduce your debt. If you are in serious trouble with debt, you will benefit from speaking to a financial advisor who will be able to assist you in getting consolidation products such as a loan to cover all of your current lines of credit and merge them all into one repayment rather than multiple ones.

Consolidating your debts can help to declutter your credit, and rather than keeping up with a number of repayments each month you will have the less stressful option of making one simple repayment for everything which you owe.

Save Money

If you find that you are constantly stressing about the amount of money which you have available and worry about what you would do financially if you were ever caught in an emergency, setting up a savings account and a system to save money can help to significantly reduce these feelings of stress and anxiety. Saving money doesn't have to be difficult – it can be something as simple as putting the $5 which you'd normally spend on coffee each morning into a savings account instead. In order to effectively save money, it's crucial to scale back your spending and work out which expenses are necessary and which are not. Take a record of your spending for a month and go through it to determine where you can make cuts and save money instead. Often, there are a range of cheaper alternatives available where you will be able to save money without losing out – such as switching to shopping at a cheaper grocery store.

Benefits of Organized Finances

Getting your finances in order, tackling your debts and saving money can help you to feel more in control which in turn has a direct effect on your happiness and well-being. Many individuals who have financial problems can feel that their money has a level of control over them, leading them to feel depressed, stressed out and hopeless. Taking this control back can eliminate the negative feelings which you have regarding your bank account and credit.

Not only that, but being able to successfully save money can give you a great sense of achievement and also help to boost your self-esteem. The feeling of achievement which people get from being able to meet a savings goal is highly satisfying and has a direct effect on how good you feel about yourself and your ability to manage your money. If managing your money is something that you struggle with, it might be worth consulting an advisor for regular help and advice.

CHAPTER 9

REMOVE TOXIC PEOPLE

Toxic people are those people in your life who always seem to add drama and create stress. Toxic people could be at your workplace, family members, or even friends who always tend to cause more problems in your life and trigger feeling of anxiety, stress or even depression when you communicate with them.

Recognizing and removing the toxic people from your life whenever possible is vital to your own happiness and well-being. Toxic people are usually chronically unhappy, and hold feelings of resentment, jealousy or frustration towards you, often due to their own mental state and not as a result of something which you have done or said to them.

Toxic people can suck the happiness out of you, and their attitudes, manipulation and even downright cruelty can leave you feeling guilty, ashamed, and unhappy. Toxic people are one of the biggest threats to your happiness, which is why determining who they are and distancing yourself from them is vital to ensure that you don't fall victim to sabotage.

Toxic People vs. Difficult People

The word 'toxic' gets overused a lot of the time these days, so it's important to be clear about what we mean by a toxic person. In life you're always going to come across people who can be a bit of a drag – perhaps you have a friend who's a bit annoying or work with a colleague who can sometimes be rude or unpleasant. This doesn't necessarily mean that a person is 'toxic' – there's a difference, and some people are simply difficult or generally undesirable.

It's important to put a bit of distance between yourself and this group of people, but there won't be the same type of urgency to cut them out of your life as there is with those individuals who are deemed toxic.

Controlling

Controlling people tend to be one of the most common types of toxic people you could find in your life. As strange as it may sound, people who have little control over their own lives try to claim back the feeling of control that they're lacking by taking control of the life of somebody else. Toxic individuals look for different ways to control others, often by using methods of manipulation such as making you feel guilty for saying no to them.

Disregard

If you know a person who has a constant disregard for your boundaries, this person is most likely toxic and will be contributing to your unhappy mental state. If you have a friend, family member or even co-worker who consistently continues to ignore you when you ask them not to do something, that person is probably toxic. Well-adjusted adults tend to find it easy and natural to respect the boundaries of others, whilst the toxic find ways to violate and override them.

Constant Taking

With any healthy relationship, there is some give and some take. Whether it be family members, friends or colleagues, a well-adjusted relationship will involve each party both giving and taking the benefits from the partnership. Give and take is the lifeblood of a good friendship or relationship.

Sometimes it's you who needs a hand, sometimes it's the other party – and both are willing to help when needed, evening it out in the end. However, toxic people don't work like this.

Rather than return the favor when needed, a toxic person will be out to take whatever they can from you without considering reciprocating your goodwill.

The Effects of Toxic People

If any of the above sounds familiar, it's highly likely that you have a toxic person in your life. The level of risk to your happiness and well-being will depend on how close you are to the person in question – for example, if there's a toxic person in your workplace who you speak to infrequently it's unlikely that they'll be a threat to your well-being. But, if the toxic person in your life is your spouse, for example, they could seriously sabotage your success and slow your progress.

Under the influence of a toxic person, you might second-guess yourself on an important decision and you'll likely experience heightened feelings of upset, sadness and discomfort. You may even begin to blame yourself and begin to feel ashamed of your progress and well-being. You could even begin to display some of the toxic qualities that you resent, as toxic people have a peculiar way of influencing others to act like them.

Removing The Toxicity

Some toxic people are more difficult to remove from your life than others. Removing toxic people from your life often has a tendency to blow up in your face and create more stress, which is why it's important for you to be prepared and accept that it will be a process that might take time.

No matter who you are cutting from your life, it's vital that you understand that it is for the best. If a person has been truly causing your happiness to diminish, they no longer deserve to play a part in your story. It's important to understand that toxic people are likely to come back even after you tell them to go away – after all, if they've never respected your boundaries before, they're not going to start now. Bear in mind that distancing yourself is a gradual process.

CHAPTER 10

CREATING A PERSONALIZED PLAN
AND PUTTING IT INTO ACTION

Hopefully, by now you will have all the information that you need in order to scale back, declutter your life, mind, diet and relationships and be on your way to a happier, more fulfilled life with less stress and anxiety.

The step which you need to take now is to create a personalized plan of action. This includes taking the methods which you have learned in this book, and applying them to your own personal situation in order to ensure that you get the most from the information. For example, you could schedule weekly mindfulness meditation sessions at a time which suits you or discuss with a financial advisor about the best way to tackle your individual debts.

When you put together a personalized plan, you should remember that it revolves around one person – you. Take the time to sit down and go through the content of this book and tailor each point to your own life to make sure that the steps which you take will be the most effective.

Writing down your plan is a great way to make sure that you're in the best position to follow it and ultimately achieve your goal. Grab a notebook and jot down everything which you plan to do to scale back and declutter in the order of importance that each strategy has to you. Put your plan somewhere that you can easily see it, such as sticking it on the refrigerator door so that you can read it each morning and remind yourself of the important journey which you are embarking on.

Conclusion & Recap

You now have all of the information that you need to declutter, scale back and become a happier person. We've covered how to accept your situation, change your mindset to become more positive, the benefits of scaling back your technology use, how to declutter your physical surroundings, the benefits of practicing meditation and gratitude daily, how your diet can affect your well-being, how to take back control of your finances, and how to recognize toxic people and remove them from your life.

Now, it's up to you to put all of these factors into action and make the essential changes to your life to enable you to become more at peace with yourself and strike the negative feelings from your mind. To get you started, here is an example action plan – in no particular order - which you may like to use as a guide.

- Each morning, start the day by remembering at least two things which you are thankful for. Repeat the process each night before you go to sleep.

- Designate a specific and certain amount of time per day to decluttering your surroundings and make this a habit to ensure that your environment remains tidy and free of clutter.

- Learn how to meditate, and schedule a time each day for this purpose.

- When you next write a grocery list, reduce the amount of processed foods and opt for the foods we've suggested.

- Consult a financial advisor, or contact any creditors about debts which worry you.

- Schedule at least one morning a week where you ban as much technology use as possible.

- Begin to distance yourself from people who you recognize as toxic.

Remember that your journey to happiness and fulfilment is personal to you.

IMPORTANT: To help you further take action, print out a copy of the *Checklist* and *Mindmap* I provided. You'll also find a Resource Cheat Sheet with valuable sites, posts and articles that I recommend you go through.